E. Glennie Jan '05

Cannich Bridge Primary School
Cannich
Beauly
inverness IV4 7LN

A first guide to

◆

Japan

By Kath Davies

A ZOË BOOK

A ZOË BOOK

© 1995 Zoë Books Limited

Devised and produced by
Zoë Books Limited
15 Worthy Lane
Winchester
Hampshire SO23 7AB
England

Illustrative material used in this book first appeared in *Discovering Japan*, published by Zoë Books Limited.

First published in Great Britain in 1995 by
Zoë Books Limited
15 Worthy Lane
Winchester
Hampshire SO23 7AB

A record of the CIP data is available from the British Library.

ISBN 1 874488 38 X

Printed in Italy by Grafedit SpA
Design: Jan Sterling, Sterling Associates
Editor: Denise Allard
Picture research: Suzanne Williams
Map: Gecko Limited
Production: Grahame Griffiths

Photographic acknowledgments

The publishers wish to acknowledge, with thanks, the following photographic sources:

Cover: Zefa; title page: Zefa; 5l Robert Harding Picture Library/Carol Jopp; 5r Robert Harding Picture Library/Nigel Blythe; 6 Robert Harding Picture Library; 7l The Hutchison Library/Jon Burbank; 7r Zefa; 8 Impact Photos/Michael Gover; 9l, 9r, 10 Zefa; 11t Werner Forman Archive/Burke Collection, New York; 11b Michael Holford; 12 The Hutchison Library/Michael MacIntyre; 13l The Hutchison Library; 13r Robert Harding Picture Library/Paul van Riel; 14 Robert Harding Picture Library/Nigel Blythe; 15l David Lewis; 15r Impact Photos/Mark Cator; 16 Robert Harding Picture Library; 17l The Hutchison Library/Jon Burbank; 17r Robert Harding Picture Library/Robert McLeod; 18 Impact Photos/Mark Cator; 19l Robert Harding Picture Library; 19r The Hutchison Library; 20 Zefa; 21l The Hutchison Library/R. Ian Lloyd; 21r Robert Harding Picture Library/Robert McLeod; 22 The Hutchison Library/Jon Burbank; 23tl Zefa; 23bl & r Robert Harding Picture Library; 24 Zefa; 25l The Hutchison Library/Jon Burbank; 25r Robert Harding Picture Library; 26 Syndication International; 27l & r The Hutchison Library/Michael MacIntyre; 28 Roger Ressmeyer, Starlight/Science Photo Library; 29l The Hutchison Library; 29r Nasda/Science Photo Library

Cover: *A Japanese girl in a* kimono

Title page: *Mount Fuji with cherry blossom*

Contents

Japanese words are shown in *italics* and are explained in the text.

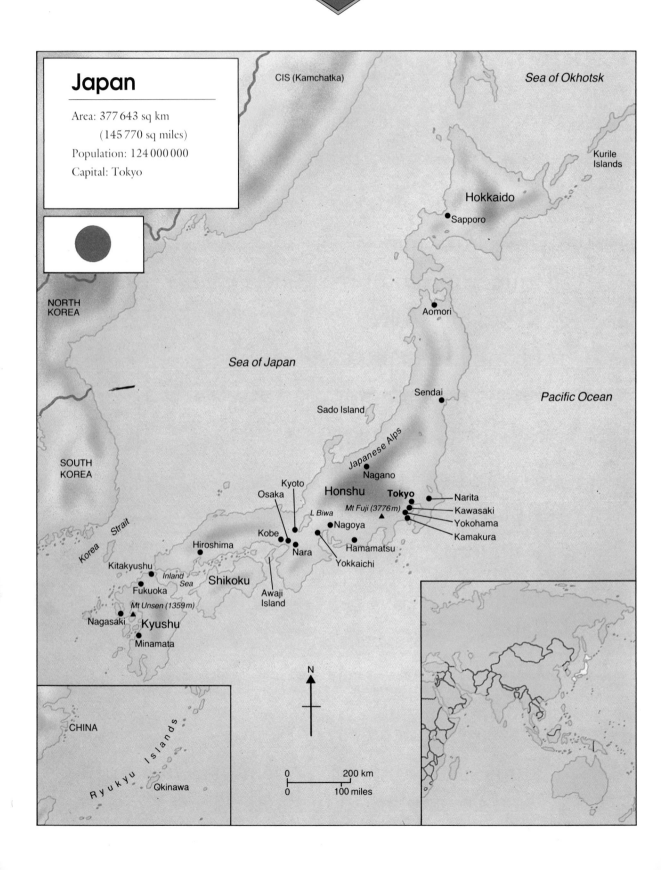

Japan

Area: 377 643 sq km
(145 770 sq miles)
Population: 124 000 000
Capital: Tokyo

CIS (Kamchatka)

Sea of Okhotsk

Kurile
Islands

Hokkaido

● Sapporo

NORTH
KOREA

Aomori

Sea of Japan

Pacific Ocean

Sado Island

● Sendai

SOUTH
KOREA

Japanese Alps

● Nagano

Kyoto

Honshu

Osaka

Tokyo

● Narita

Mt Fuji (3776 m)

● Kawasaki

L Biwa

● Yokohama

Kobe

● Nagoya

● Kamakura

Hiroshima

Nara

Hamamatsu

Korea

Yokkaichi

Strait

Kitakyushu

Inland

Shikoku

Sea

Fukuoka

Awaji
Island

Mt Unsen (1359 m)

Nagasaki

Kyushu

● Minamata

N

CHINA

R y u k y u I s l a n d s

Okinawa

0   200 km

0   100 miles

Welcome!

Yookoso – Welcome to Japan! The people of Japan call their country, 'the land of the rising sun', or *Nihon* in Japanese.

Japan is made up of about 4000 islands. The four largest islands are Hokkaido, Honshu, Shikoku and Kyushu. These long, narrow islands stretch for 3500 kilometres (2000 miles) in the Pacific Ocean.

High mountains cover most of the islands. In winter there is snow in the northern areas and on these mountains.

▼ Autumn in the mountains

▲ People go to see the blossom.

More than 124 million people live in Japan. Most of them live in the flat lands near the coasts, or in the deep valleys.

Spring is mild. Japanese people love the blossom on the fruit trees. There is plenty of rain. The summers are very hot and damp. In autumn the leaves turn red and yellow. Winters can be very cold.

The people of Japan

Most of the people who live in Japan are Japanese. About 150 000 Chinese people also live in Japan, and some Koreans. Many people go to Japan to work, but they do not have the right to stay there.

The Japanese language has strict rules. Women may use some words which men may not. Other words are used only by men.

There are also special words which people use when they are being polite to each other. People who learn Japanese must be very careful not to use the wrong words!

▼ Street signs in Tokyo

▲ Learning to write *kanji*

All Japanese children learn English at school for six years. They can read English, but they do not often speak the language.

Writing

Japanese people did not have their own way of writing until about 1000 years ago. Before that time, they used Chinese writing. Chinese people write pictures or signs for words. These signs are called *kanji*.

Japanese people now use *kanji*, which has about 2000 signs, and also two sets of marks called *kana*.

People write from the top to the bottom of a page, and from right to left.

Giving gifts

In Japan, giving gifts is an important part of life. People give each other presents in the middle of the year, and at the end of it. This is to say 'thank you' to people at work, and to neighbours.

People also give gifts for birthdays, and when they go on visits. The gifts are wrapped and tied with ribbons. At the New Year, or for happy events, the ribbons are red or gold.

▼ Shopping for gifts

Travel in Japan

In Japan's big cities, traffic jams are very bad. They sometimes stretch for 48 kilometres (about 30 miles). More than 12 million people live in Tokyo, the capital of Japan. Each day, another three million people come into the city to work. Most people travel by bicycle and by train. The trains are very crowded.

The main railway company in Japan is the Japan Railways Group (JR). It runs 26 000 trains every day. Some trains have two decks of seats. There are TV sets on the top deck.

▼ Rush hour in Tokyo

Railways were first built about 100 years ago. Before that time, the easiest way to travel was by boat. Ferries still sail amongst the four main islands of Japan, and the six biggest cities are all on the coast.

The fastest trains in Japan are called 'bullet trains', the *shinkansen*. They can travel at up to 275 kph (170 mph). Another fast train is now being built. It is called the *Maglev*. This train does not have wheels. Instead, it is pulled along a special track by a magnet.

▼ A 'bullet train' passes Mount Fuji

Tunnels and bridges

Bridges link many of Japan's islands. The world's longest

▲ The city harbour at Kobe

suspension bridge will soon link Kobe city to Awaji island. It will be nearly 4 km (2.5 miles) long. The longest sea tunnel runs between Honshu and Hokkaido. It is 54 km (33.5 miles) long, and is called the Seikan Tunnel.

Air travel

There are more than 60 airports in Japan. In 1994 the Kansai International Airport opened. First the builders made a new island in Osaka Bay. Then they built the airport on the island.

The bird called a crane means good luck in Japan. A red crane is the symbol of Japan Airlines.

Emperors, empresses and *shoguns*

▲ A temple at Nara

More than 12 000 years ago, people called the Ainu lived in Japan. Then people from China and northeast Asia pushed them to the north. Today, about 24 000 Ainu people still live in Hokkaido. The earliest writings which tell us about Japan are 1700 years old. They say that at that time, Japan had women rulers.

No one knows when the first emperors and empresses ruled. For about 1500 years, Japan's rulers have come from the same family.

About 1175 years ago, the emperor Kammu built a capital city, called Heiankyo, or 'capital of peace'. It was Japan's capital city until 1863. Today the city is called Kyoto.

▲ A *shogun's* castle

The *shoguns*

The royal family stayed in Kyoto, while rich families fought for power. About 800 years ago, the Genji family ruled Japan through its army leader, the *shogun*. *Shoguns* were the real rulers for about 700 years.

A closed country

European people arrived in Japan about 400 years ago. Some of them wanted to buy and sell goods. They were traders from Holland and Portugal. Other people came to tell the Japanese about the religion of Christianity.

The *shoguns* were afraid of the travellers' new ideas. After 1603, no one was allowed into or out of Japan without their permission. In 1854 the *shoguns* allowed people to trade with Japan. Ten years later, the *shoguns* had lost their power.

▼ Europeans arrive in Japan

Kyoto and Tokyo

Tokyo is now the capital of Japan. Before the year 1868, Kyoto was the capital for 1000 years. Kyoto was once the home of the emperors and empresses of Japan. The city became a centre for arts, crafts and religion.

There are 1600 temples in Kyoto. They are part of the religion called Buddhism. The Shinto religion also has 270 holy places, or shrines, in Kyoto. They are decorated with carved wood, and stone and bronze statues.

Kyoto is still a religious centre, but today it is also a modern city with important electronic industries.

▼ The 'crane dance' at a shrine in Kyoto

▲ A puppet show in Tokyo

Japanese theatre

There are four types of theatre in Japan today.

Actors wear masks to take part in the song and dance act called *Noh*. There are also short comedies called *Kyogen*. The name means 'crazy speech'. Both these styles of acting are 600 years old.

About 400 years ago, a puppet show called *Bunraku* appeared. Three people move each puppet. At about the same time, a religious dance called *Kabuki* was started by nuns. When women were not allowed to work in the theatre, men dressed up to play their parts.

Tokyo

Tokyo's name means 'eastern capital'. The city was called Edo until 1868. Then the *shoguns'* castle became the Imperial Palace. Edo became Tokyo, the capital of Japan.

Many of the old buildings in Tokyo were destroyed during the Second World War. Tokyo is now a huge modern city. It is the centre of government, politics, fashion and art.

▼ The town hall at Shinjuku, Tokyo

Living in Japan

About 50 years ago many homes in cities were destroyed. This happened during the Second World War. New homes were built quickly. There was not much space in the crowded cities, so most houses were small. Today, most people live in new flats in the cities.

Japanese homes have a hall, or *genkan*, where outdoor shoes are kept. People wear slippers or socks inside. The main room may have mats made from rice straw, *tatami*, on the floor. Rooms can be divided by screens for different uses. At night, bedding is laid on the floor. Children sometimes sleep in bunk beds to save space. A Japanese bath is hot and deep. People shower first, then relax in the bath.

▼ A family meal at home

Enjoy yourself!

Almost all Japanese homes have a television set. People enjoy music, and all kinds of games. Sports are also popular.

After work, many people go to bars. They like to sing to recorded music. They hold a microphone, and sing songs to the people in the bar. This is called *karaoke*, which means 'empty orchestra'.

Pachinko is a pinball game. Players sit in rows at the machines.

▼ People playing *pachinko*

▲ Baseball practice in Tokyo

Sports

Baseball is the most popular sport in Japan. Twelve teams play in national competitions. It is also played at school. Everyone watches the final of the schools contest on television.

Golf is also popular. People practise in multi-storey golf buildings, because there is not much space for golf courses.

Sumo wrestling is the national sport of Japan. It is at least 1700 years old. Wrestlers train from the age of fifteen. They eat special foods, so that they grow very big and heavy.

Food and shopping

Japanese people eat rice at almost every meal. The Japanese word for breakfast means 'morning rice'. Lunch is 'noon rice' and dinner is 'evening rice'. Rice is made into cakes for special events, and into rice wine, called *sake*.

The Japanese often eat raw fish, called *sashimi*. Another dish is made from seaweed. People do not eat much meat, because there are not many sheep or cattle. The people who brought the religion of Buddhism to Japan did not eat meat. This is part of their religion. So Japanese people are used to this way of eating. Most meals include soy beans which are used in foods such as soup (*miso*) or curd (*tofu*).

▼ Models of food which is served at a restaurant

▲ A family meal of raw fish

Popular foods

Some shops sell noodles called *soba* and *udon*, which are eaten with soup. Food is eaten in the shop or taken away.

Other bars sell dishes of raw fish, called *sushi*. Customers help themselves from dishes on a moving counter.

Street sellers

Street stalls, called *yatai*, sell freshly cooked food. Every evening, food stalls are put up on the streets. There are also machines on the streets, where people can buy food.

Shopping

Most shops in Japan are open from 10am to 7pm. They open on Saturdays and Sundays, but they close for one day each week. Some food shops are open 24 hours a day.

In large cities there are underground shops. Many big stores run evening classes and hold art exhibitions.

▼ A market stall in Tokyo

School and work

Japanese children start school when they are six years old. At the age of 15, almost all pupils go on to Senior High School. About half the students go to college or to university.

▲ Central Tokyo Junior High School

Children work hard at school. The schools choose which children may go to them. The children have to take a test for this. Everyone tries to get into the best schools.

School starts at 8.30 am and ends at 3.30 pm. Children go to school on Saturdays, but they leave earlier. There is no school on Sundays.

▲ Prayers for good luck in tests

After school

In the afternoons, most children go to clubs or to private schools, called *juku*. They have extra lessons to help them to pass their tests. At the clubs, they play baseball or learn to play music. At home, they do two or three hours of homework.

Martial arts (*ninja*)

Japanese soldiers, called *samurai*, had many fighting skills. These are called martial arts, or *ninja*. Many children learn these at *juku*.

Work

Most people in Japan work long hours. They may travel for up to two hours from home to work. When people start a job, they learn all about the company. They also learn about bowing. It is an important part of working life.

In many factories and offices, the day begins with exercises. The workers bow to each other, and sing the company's song.

▲ Daily exercises

Women at work

In the past, if Japanese women had children, they often did not work outside the home. Today more women go out to work, and many have very good jobs.

Where people work

Japan makes all types of goods, especially electrical goods, cars, cameras and computers. It is one of the most important industrial countries of the world. Most homes in Europe, North America and Australia have some Japanese goods. The names of companies such as Honda, Sony and Toshiba are known all over the world. The factories at Toyota city on Honshu island make four million cars a year.

Some of the factories use robots to help with the work. There are more than 300 000 robots in Japanese factories.

Many factories used to pour chemicals into the sea. Now the sea has been poisoned, or polluted, in some areas. Today, there are laws which try to stop people polluting the air and the sea.

▼ A car factory at Hiroshima

▲ Rice fields in northern Honshu

Farming and fishing

Most farms in Japan are very small, so farming families usually work at other jobs, too. Rice is an important crop. Farmers also grow vegetables and fruit.

The Japanese catch more fish than any other country. Herring and sardines are found near the coast. Fishing boats also sail to the Arctic and Antarctic Oceans.

Buying materials

Almost all the material which people need to make goods has to be bought from other countries. Japan has plenty of water and trees, but not many other natural resources.

Some iron ore for steel-making comes from India and Australia.

Energy

Energy is needed in factories to make the machines work. Most electricity is made from oil and coal. Japan buys oil from China, Mexico and the Middle East. It buys coal from Australia, the USA and Canada.

There are 39 nuclear power stations in Japan. Many people fear nuclear accidents, so they are against using this power.

▼ Unloading fish

Holidays and festivals

Schools close for six weeks in the summer. Workers, however, may have only two weeks holiday a year. There are also 13 national holidays. Three of these are in the first week of May, which is called Golden Week. Another busy holiday is New Year, when most offices close for one week.

People enjoy going to the beach on Sundays in the summer. Many people also go to the mountains. There are places called *onsen* where people relax in hot springs of water. In winter, the ski resorts in the Japanese Alps, and on Hokkaido island, are very popular.

In August, the festival called *o-bon* is for members of the family who have died. People light bonfires, and dance in the streets.

▼ A beach in summer

▲ Hot springs in the mountains

Some national holidays

  1 Jan - New Year's Day
 15 Jan - Coming of Age Day
 11 Feb - National Foundation
 21 Mar - Spring Equinox
  3 May - Constitution Day
  5 May - Children's Day
 15 Sep - Respect for the Aged
 10 Oct - Health and Sport Day
  3 Nov - Culture Day
 23 Nov - Thanks for Work Day

▼ The snow festival at Sapporo

For children

On the seventh night of the seventh month (7 July), the star festival is held. Children write poems and tie them to bamboo branches.

There is a special day in November. It is for girls who are seven or three years old, and boys who are five. It is called 7-5-3, *Shichi-go-san*. The children dress in their best clothes, or in *kimonos*.

▼ Wearing *kimonos* for a festival

Religion in Japan

The most popular religions in Japan are Shinto and Buddhism. Many Japanese people follow both faiths. Weddings and the arrival of babies are blessed at Shinto shrines. Funerals are held in Buddhist temples.

Shinto is the oldest religion in Japan. The name means, 'the way of the gods'. People believe that the sun, trees and mountains are gods.

Shinto shrines are calm, beautiful places. They have red gateways called *torii*. Stone animals guard the way into the shrine. There is a place to wash, and a wooden box for money. Visitors read their fortune on a piece of paper. If it is not good, they tie the paper to a tree and leave it behind!

▼ The gateway to a shrine

▲ A Buddhist temple 'dragon dance'

Buddhism

Buddhism was brought to Japan by holy people called monks. They followed the teaching of an Indian prince called the Buddha. The monks came to Japan about 1500 years ago. New ideas, called Zen Buddhism, arrived about 400 years later. Zen monks brought the tea ceremony to Japan. They made gardens with rocks, where they could be quiet and think in peace.

Confucius

Confucius was a writer and teacher. He lived about 2500 years ago. Japanese people still read and follow his ideas.

Christianity

A Spanish priest brought Christianity to Japan about 450 years ago. His name was St Francis Xavier, and his followers are called Jesuits. Christianity was banned for about 300 years. There are now about one million Christians in Japan.

▼ A statue of the Buddha

Japan at war

In 1894, Japan went to war with China and won. It was the first time that Japan had fought any other country. The two countries wanted power over another country, Korea.

In 1904, Japan fought Russia, and won again. This time, Japan wanted to control Manchuria. These wars were fought because Japan needed coal, iron ore and oil from the other countries, for its own industries.

After these wars, Japan's industries grew, and so did the number of people living in Japan. Many people went to live in the USA. The US government stopped Japanese people from living in America. This angered Japan.

▼ Hiroshima, after the atomic bomb

▲ Self Defence Forces

In 1941, Japan entered the Second World War. It bombed US ships at Pearl Harbor in the Pacific. Fighting went on for four years.

The first atomic bombs

At the end of the Second World War, two American atomic bombs were dropped on Japan. The bomb that exploded over the town of Hiroshima on 6 August 1945 killed 78 000 people. It injured 30 000 others. Another atomic bomb killed 45 000 people in Nagasaki on 11 August.

On 15 August 1945, the Japanese surrendered.

After the war

Japan had been conquered for the first time. US soldiers and other people stayed there until 1952. The Americans helped the Japanese people to recover from the war. Changes were made to the rules about how Japan was governed. These rules are called a Constitution.

Japan's Constitution says that the people will not fight outside the country. Japan has no army, but it does train soldiers. They are the Self Defence Forces.

▼ A march against nuclear power

Japan today

It is only about 125 years since Japan was closed to the outside world. Now it buys materials, energy and food from many other countries. Japan has become a rich country by selling its goods at home and all over the world.

▲ The Space Centre at Isukuba

Almost half of Japan's trade is with Europe, North America and Australia. Japanese companies now have factories in these areas. They provide jobs for many people.

▲ Old people pray at a temple

Old people in Japan

Japanese people can expect to live longer than anyone else in the world.

Families are smaller now in Japan. This means that soon there will be more old people than young ones in Japan.

More land

Japan needs more space for its people. It has agreed to help Russia with money and technology. In return, it wants two of the Kurile islands, which are ruled by Russia, to be given back to Japan.

Whaling

In the past, Japan caught more whales than any other country. Today, there is a ban on killing whales. People come to the Ogasawara islands to watch whales, not to kill them.

The space race

Japanese scientists joined in space exploration in 1970. Their rockets were American. Now the US buys Japanese engines for its rockets.

▼ A rocket launch at Osaki

Fact file

Government

Japan has emperors and empresses, who do not rule. Parliament, called the Diet, makes laws to govern Japan. There are about 700 Members of Parliament (MPs), and two Houses. They are the House of Councillors and the House of Representatives. The people elect the MPs, and the MPs choose the Prime Minister.

Flag

Japan's flag is white with a red circle in the middle. The circle stands for the sun. The Chinese called Japan *Nihon*, 'the land of the rising sun'. The name 'Japan' came from a European traveller, Marco Polo, about 700 years ago.

National anthem

The words of the national song, or anthem, come from a poem which is 1000 years old. It is called *Kimigayo*, which means, 'His Majesty's reign'. It was first set to music in 1880.

Religion

More than 100 million people in Japan follow the Shinto religion. About 91 million people are Buddhists. Many people follow both faiths.

Money

Japanese money is called the *yen*. The name comes from a Chinese word which means 'round' and 'a dollar'.

Education

All Japanese children go to their first school for six years. They then go on to Junior High School for three years. Most of them study at Senior High School for another three years. More than 2 million pupils study at a college or university. There are 500 universities in Japan. Most of them are not run by the state.

Some famous people

Japanese names have the surname first.

Murasaki Shikibu (?978-1014) wrote one of the world's first novels, *The Tale of Genji*.

Katsushika Hokusai (1760-1849) was an artist. His work made the Japanese style popular in Europe.

Kano Jigoro (1860-1938) developed the sport of judo.

Yamamato Isoroku (1884-1943) was the naval leader who attacked Pearl Harbor.

Ichikawa Fusae (1893-1981) led the campaign to give women the vote in Japan.

Tomonaga Shin'ichiro (1906-) won the Nobel prize for physics in 1965.

Kurosawa Akira (1910-) is a world-famous film director.

Mishima Yukio (1925-70) wrote plays and novels.

Miyake Issey (1938-) is a fashion designer.

Some key events in history

AD400s: the most powerful Japanese families joined to form the Yamato state.

710: first capital at Nara.

794: capital moved to Kyoto.

1185: Yoritomo became the first *shogun*.

1542: Portugese sailors arrived in Japan.

1549: arrival of Christianity in Japan.

1616-1853: no contact with the outside world.

1853: US ships arrived.

1858: Japan opened some ports to trade.

1868: rule of *shoguns* ended. Emperor moved to Edo. Edo renamed Tokyo.

1894: war with China.

1904: war with Russia.

1941: Japan joined the Second World War.

1945: atomic bombs over Hiroshima and Nagasaki.

Index